Mountain Dance

THOMAS LOCKER

SILVER WHISTLE

HARCOURT, INC.

San Diego   New York   London

Manufactured in China

MOUNTAINS RISE through the clouds
in a slow dance that goes on and on
for millions of years.
Every kind of mountain moves in its own way.

Slumbering volcanoes awake, roaring.

Fire, gas, and ash leap.

Cone-shaped mountains rise from the land.

In the middle of the sea, quiet shield volcanoes
steadily ooze streams of boiling, hissing lava.
Volcanic islands build up from the ocean's floor.

Near cracks in the earth's crust,
jagged fault-block mountains
lift and sink, lean and bend.

Shy dome mountains bubble up
underneath older mountains.
The domes hide for millions of years
until the rocks above are worn away
by wind, water, and ice.

Folded mountains dip down
and well up like waves
flowing across the land.

Mountains rarely appear alone.
They dance in long lines that go on and on
as far as the eye can see.

But even the most rugged mountain
does not last forever.
The hardest stone can be worn down
by wind, water, and weather.

When the earth turns cold,
rivers of glacial ice grind and flatten mountains
into hills and plains.

When the earth is warm,
hot winds can sandblast mountains
into crumbling stone sculptures.

Year after year,

mountain streams carry stone,

broken by the forces of nature,

into rivers that end in the sea.

Beneath the sea,
stone piles up.
When the sea recedes,
deltas emerge,
becoming erosion mountains.

Beneath the stars,
mountains dance their slow dance
that goes on and on
in the endless beauty of the universe.

ABOUT MOUNTAINS

IN THE EARLY twentieth century, when scientists and explorers reached the top of Mount Everest, more than five miles above sea level on the border of China and Nepal, they were amazed to find the fossils of sea creatures. How did a sea creature get to the top of a mountain? By studying the different kinds of mountains and the ways they form, we can discover the answer to this puzzle.

VOLCANO

Most kinds of mountains take millions of years to form. Volcanoes, however, can rise up suddenly and explosively. Fifty years ago, a Mexican farmer noticed steam rising from his field. A volcano erupted. Melted stone called lava, hot cinders, and ash shot upward. The lava hardened as it cooled. After a few weeks, instead of a field, there stood a volcano higher than some skyscrapers. Sometimes the sound of an eruption is so loud that it can be heard for hundreds of miles. The ash thrown up into the sky creates brilliant sunsets.

SHIELD VOLCANO

Most volcanoes are found on land near the sea, where parts of the earth's crust collide. But many volcanoes form under the sea. Some volcanoes occur when one rock plate below the earth slides under another plate. Heat and pressure force the rock upward toward the earth's surface. In the middle of the Pacific Ocean is a chain of islands that includes the Hawaiian Islands. The chain stretches for more than a thousand miles. Each island was formed above a hot spot vent connecting the surface of the earth to its hot, fluid inner layer. As the crust moves over the fixed hot spot, molasses-like lava oozes up and cools. It builds layer upon layer of hardened stone. In this quiet, steady way, volcanic islands, like the shields of ancient warriors, grow.

FAULT BLOCK

It is easy to understand how the earth's hot inner zone helps build volcanoes. But the heat and pressure caused by the magma, the melted stone within the earth, is also active in the creation of other types of mountains. In some places, this pressure can stretch and push at the earth's crust until long cracks, called faults, occur. Between the faults, the crust forms blocks. On one side of the fault, the block might slide downward, upward, sideways, or it may be shoved upon the neighboring block. The jagged Teton Range of Wyoming and the eastern part of the Sierra Nevada of California are examples of fault-block mountains.

DOME

The upward pressure caused by the magma doesn't always pierce or crack the earth's crust. It may just create pockets of very dense stone sandwiched between the magma below and the softer rock above. These dome- or bubble-shaped formations remain hidden until the softer stone above is worn away by wind or water erosion. The Black Hills of South Dakota, some mountains in Yosemite National Park in California, and the Adirondack Mountains of New York are examples of dome mountains.

FOLDED MOUNTAINS

Folded mountains are the result of the movement or squeezing together of the earth's crust. The parts of the crust, called plates, sometimes move in colliding directions deep below the earth's surface. When one plate pushes against another, folds appear. When gigantic plates collide, tall folds rise up. The Himalayas were formed by a collision between the Indian plate and the Eurasian plate. Fossils of oceanic creatures were in the uplifted stone. That is the answer to our puzzle.

RANGES

Mountains are usually parts of long lines of mountains called ranges. Mount Everest is part of the Himalayan range. Mauna Kea is part of a range, with many of the mountains underwater, that extends for more than a thousand miles. The Rocky Mountains are part of a chain that begins in Alaska and extends all the way to Central America. The Rocky Mountains include examples of most of the different types of mountains.

EROSION

ICE EROSION

WIND EROSION

WATER EROSION

Soaring stone mountains seem solid, heavy, and permanent. They look like they could last forever, but they don't. Mountains are worn down by the changing forces of nature. The Himalayas, for instance, began rising long after the dinosaurs disappeared. These mountains continue growing at about one centimeter a year. Someday, when the forces of erosion become stronger than the growth caused by the folding, they may stop growing and wear away.

The earth's climate has changed many times during its history. At some points in time, the earth was quite warm; at other times, it was quite cool. During cool periods, like the last Ice Age, which began a million years ago and ended about twelve thousand years ago, great sheets of ice, called glaciers, formed. They covered parts of North America, Europe, and Asia. Glaciers still exist at and near the northern- and southernmost poles of the earth. Moving glacial ice, carrying rocks and sand, can break stone and transport it as it smoothes and flattens mountains in its path. Retreating glaciers sometimes leave behind hills created by the stone and earth once held by the ice. Someday the world will cool and the earth-shaping glaciers will return.

During warm cycles in the earth's changing climate, wind erodes mountains. Wind picks up sand and hurls it. Bit by bit the sandblasting carves stone. In the desert, there are strange monumental sculptures. Long ago they were big slabs of flat-lying sedimentary rock. After years of carving by sandblasting wind, they took shapes. The rest is blown away by the wind.

Water can move mountains. Water can dissolve more substances than any other liquid. Water trickles into cracks in stone and then sometimes freezes. When it freezes, it expands, breaking the stone. Mountain streams carry sand and bits of stone that grind away, making deeper rivers. The water also carries some materials into the sea.

EROSION MOUNTAINS

When the river waters enter the salt water of the sea, the tiny bits of stone and dissolved minerals are deposited on underwater deltas. When the earth's climate changes or the land under the delta is uplifted, the delta becomes a plateau that is called an erosion mountain. The Pocono Mountains of Pennsylvania and the Catskill Mountains of New York are examples of erosion mountains.

Beneath the endless stars, continents drift. Mountains rise up and bow down. Stone is recycled by the ever changing earth, and new mountains rise. It goes on and on for millions of years. But the slow dance of the mountains is just a brief moment, a blink of an eye, in the vast history of the universe.

Scientific information was written with the assistance of Candace Christiansen, children's book author and science teacher, and Dr. Donald Fisher, Geologist (retired), New York Geological Survey and State Museum, Albany, New York.

To Zoë and Korinne
—T. L.

Requests for permission to make copies of any part of the work
should be mailed to the following address:
Permissions Department, Harcourt, Inc.,
6277 Sea Harbor Drive, Orlando, Florida 32887-6777.

www.harcourt.com

Silver Whistle is a trademark of Harcourt, Inc., registered in the
United States of America and/or other jurisdictions.

Library of Congress Cataloging-in-Publication Data
Locker, Thomas, 1937–
Mountain Dance/Thomas Locker.
p.   m.
"Silver Whistle."
Summary: A poetic description of various kinds of mountains and
how they are formed. Includes factual information on mountains.
[1. Mountains—Fiction.]   I. Title.
PZ7.L7945Mo   2001
[E]—dc21   00-11933
ISBN 0-15-202622-3

First edition
A C E G H F D B

The illustrations in this book were done in oils on canvas.
The display calligraphy was hand lettered by John Stevens.
The display type was set in Engravers Roman.
The text type was set in Berkeley Old Style.
Color separations by Bright Arts Ltd., Hong Kong
Manufactured by South China Printing Company, Ltd., China
This book was printed on totally chlorine-free
Nymolla Matte Art paper.
Production supervision by Sandra Grebenar and Ginger Boyer
Designed by Ivan Holmes